Original title:
The Sea's Soft Heart

Copyright © 2025 Creative Arts Management OÜ
All rights reserved.

Author: Julian Carmichael
ISBN HARDBACK: 978-1-80587-436-2
ISBN PAPERBACK: 978-1-80587-906-0

Whispers of the Tidal Embrace

The waves giggle as they play,
Tickling toes at the end of the day.
Seagulls swoop, like they've lost the bet,
Stolen fries make them a bit upset.

With each splash, a joke is told,
Shells rolling in, glimmering gold.
The crabs dance on their little feet,
Thinking they're brave, but they can't take the heat.

Echoes Beneath the Azure Waves

Bubbles rise like little dreams,
Whispering secrets in quirky themes.
Fish do the tango, fins in a twirl,
They think they're cool, but they just swirl.

A dolphin snickers, flips in the blue,
Thinking it's clever, but we all knew.
Turtles wearing shades, so chic and snazzy,
Just waiting for the sun to make them jazzy.

Secrets Cradled in Ocean's Gentle Caress

Starfish with a wink, all dressed up nice,
Playing poker on a sandy slice.
Seashells whisper gossip, oh so bold,
About the octopus stealing the gold.

Crabs argue over the best hiding spots,
While seaweed sways like tangled thoughts.
Clams clap along, their pearls in sight,
Throwing a party, shining so bright.

Lullabies on the Salted Breeze

The breeze sings softly, tickling sand,
While sandcastles rise, a marvelous stand.
But watch out, waves sneak up and say,
'Here comes a flood, and it's time to play!'

Jellyfish dance in their jelly-like suits,
Popping up, like cheeky little loots.
The tides are a prankster, pulling you near,
With a splash of laughter, they'll disappear.

Longing for the Ocean's Whispers

Sandy toes and seagulls cry,
I swear they gave me the eye.
Jumping waves, oh what a tease,
Can I ride you with such ease?

Shells sing tunes from long ago,
While jellyfish dance in the flow.
I ask a crab to join my dance,
He just stares, no second chance.

Crystalline Caresses of the Waves

Bubbles pop like whispered glee,
Their giggles echo back to me.
Surfboards wobble, splashes fly,
Caught a wave—oh me, oh my!

Starfish lounging, looking cool,
Claiming rocks like they own the pool.
I tried to join their beachy fun,
But ended up with just a sunburn.

Waves Kissing the Forgotten

Old boots washed up on the shore,
Whispers of someone who swore,
To never leave, oh what a scene,
But waves said, 'You're too mean!'

Fish come gossip, swirling round,
"Did you hear? That guy just drowned!"
I laughed so hard, I did a flip,
The ocean winked, I took a dip.

Unity in the Currents

Crabs and clams have formed a band,
With seaweed dancers lending a hand.
The rhythm's funky, waves all groove,
    Even the boats start to move!

We sway and sway till night descends,
The stars above bring all their friends.
    And as I lose my sandy beat,
The tide just laughs, 'Ain't this sweet?'

Heartstrings Tied to the Ocean's Pulse

Waves dance like jelly, full of glee,
Fish flip-flop, a sight to see.
Seagulls squawk in their funny tune,
Sandcastles sigh 'neath the laughing moon.

Crabs wear hats made of driftwood sway,
Shells whisper secrets of ocean play.
The tide sends giggles, soft as air,
While dolphins play tag without a care.

Beneath the Horizon: A Gentle Promise

Under a sun like a popping gold,
Winks at the waves, oh so bold.
Barnacles joke on a rusty chair,
Laughing at fish with fanciful hair.

Mermaids sing with a comical flare,
Splashing each other, without a care.
The horizon winks, promises delight,
As seaweed dances, holding on tight.

Tides Turning to Soft Serenades

The tide rolls in with a cheeky grin,
Who knew it could be so much fun to swim?
Stars in the sky, giggling with pride,
While pinching the beach in a great big tide.

Ocean bubbles carry tales untold,
Of sea cucumbers, brazen and bold.
Each splash is a laugh, each foam a cheer,
As the waves tease sand and pull it near.

A Shoreline of Secrets and Solace

Secrets whisper between the shells,
Crabs tell tales, swapping merry yells.
Kites fly high with a silly song,
Wind spins around, all day long.

Footprints giggle as they skip along,
Waves join in, strumming a song.
The sands hide treasures of silly dreams,
Under the sun, life oft redeems.

Echoes of Forgotten Mariner's Songs

A sailor once sang out of tune,
His voice was lost 'neath the moon.
Fish chuckled as they danced around,
While crabs tapped feet on the sandy ground.

Seashells whispered secrets so bright,
To seagulls swooping, what a sight!
A parrot squawked, 'You call that a song?'
Laughter echoed, all night long!

Currents of Kindness

A dolphin once borrowed a cap,
Said, 'Look at me! I'm a mishap!'
A wave rolled by with a gentle tease,
And jellyfish giggled in the breeze.

Turtles shared snacks like they were gold,
Eating seaweed—oh, so bold!
An octopus painted with flair and grace,
Declared, 'Who needs a regular space?'

Maritime Poetry in Motion

A crab wrote poems in the sand,
With jellyfish cheering from the strand.
They crafted verses, light and tall,
While barnacles joined the joyous call.

A buoy sighed, 'I feel so bright,'
As kites flew high, what a sight!
The gulls all joined in silly rhyme,
Making memories, one silly time!

Embracing the Ocean's Warmth

A fish wore a scarf, what a view,
Said, 'I'm chilly; how about you?'
The tide rolled in with a playful grin,
And waves laughed, 'Let the fun begin!'

An anchor dreamed of flying high,
While seagulls swooped, oh my, oh my!
The sand danced joyfully, toes a-twirl,
In the warmth of the sea's silly swirl!

Crashing Waves with a Gentle Touch

Waves crash loud then whisper light,
Tickling toes with pure delight.
Seagulls laugh, they steal a fry,
Wearing silly hats, oh my!

Water's edge, a slippery dance,
Shells play hide and seek, perchance.
A crab in boots stumbles and falls,
Sandy giggles fill the calls.

The Breath of Serenity under Stormy Skies

Clouds rumble, then they sip tea,
Breezes tease with perfect glee.
Thunder sings, a jazzy beat,
While fish wear boots to shuffle their feet.

The lighthouse twirls, a dance divine,
As waves discuss their latest line.
Splashing joy, a sloshy cheer,
They giggle loud, they have no fear.

Love Letters Written in Sea Foam

Foamy letters float on by,
Telling tales of fish who fly.
Octopuses write with flair and style,
A love note drifts, makes tides smile.

Dolphins wink, they're quite the poets,
In salty ink, the ocean knows it.
Seashells blush at every word,
Shy seagulls wish they had heard.

A Ballet of Waves and Wonder

Waves pirouette, they leap and spin,
With seashells clapping, they all chime in.
Jellyfish glide in tutus bright,
Performing under the moon's soft light.

Stars twinkle like a grand applause,
As fish in flippers flaunt their flaws.
Orcas join in – what a sight!
A splashy dance in the cool moonlight.

Where the Coral Kisses the Tides

Bubbles giggle as they rise,
Crabs wear hats, no surprise.
Starfish dance in quirky flair,
Seahorses twirl without a care.

An octopus serves fishy tea,
Clams debate who's the best sea.
Seaweed sways like it's in a show,
Mermaids laugh, putting on a glow.

The Heartbeat of the Ocean Floor

Clams keep time with a rhythmic clap,
Sandy bears take a cozy nap.
Jellyfish bounce, they float and glide,
As whispers tickle the ocean wide.

A turtle spins in a hula twist,
Waves are giggling, couldn't resist.
Fish play tag, quick as a flash,
Under blue umbrellas, they dash.

Murmurs from the Deep

Whales crack jokes, deep down low,
Mermaids hum a bubbly flow.
Eels play peek-a-boo all night,
While starry fish give a wink of light.

Squids sketch art with inky flair,
Tangs wear shades, they just don't care.
Every splash, a laugh so bright,
In the depths, it's pure delight.

Soothing Sands and Whispering Waters

Pebbles joke as they roll and sway,
Crabs tell tales of their wild day.
Seagulls cackle, they're quite the crew,
Wave after wave, they're laughing too.

Driftwood dreams in a shady spot,
Seashells gossip, believe it or not.
The tides tickle the shore with glee,
Where surf meets sand, happy as can be.

A Dance with the Nautical Spirits

The fishes throw a party tonight,
In top hats and tails, such a sight.
They invite crabs who dance with glee,
And jellyfish twirl, feeling so free.

A clam plays the drums, with shells so loud,
While seagulls squawk, all feeling proud.
The waves join in, a rhythmic embrace,
As each splash giggles in this happy space.

The Color of Water's Heartbeat

The tide wears socks of bright green kelp,
A fish in slippers says, "Oh, help!"
Whales wear bow ties, looking quite dapper,
As dolphins leap in a joyful caper.

Octopuses juggle shells in a crowd,
While starfish cheer, both noisy and loud.
Coral reefs blush in hues of delight,
As the sun dips low, ending the night.

Gentle Ripples of Nostalgia

A rubber duck floats in unparalleled style,
Winking at crabs with a cheeky smile.
Seaweed dances, like hair in the breeze,
While playful turtles slow-dip with ease.

Memories swirl like leaves in the air,
Oh, the pranks played by the old sea bear!
With each little wave, a giggle resounds,
Where laughter and joy know no bounds.

Luminous Depths of Solitude

In the depths, a sardine's having a ball,
Finding new friends, both big and small.
A pufferfish tells jokes that go 'pop',
As the shy sea cucumbers flip and flop.

Meditating squids with a peace sign pose,
Counting stars as the ocean glows.
They laugh at the moon, such a bright tease,
Floating together, they drift with the breeze.

Haiku of the Horizon's Heart

Waves whisper to me,
Fish in tuxedos swim by,
Laughing at my dive.

Seagulls play charades,
Stealing chips from picnic folks,
A flock full of tricks.

Sun wears a bright hat,
Shadows dance on golden sands,
Nature's comedy.

Shells gossip with shells,
Treasure maps sketched in the sand,
Who'll find them? Not me!

Moonbeams Dancing on the Water

Moonlight winks at waves,
Crabs wear shades, looking cool,
Who stole my last fry?

Starfish spin around,
Pointing toes like ballerinas,
Quite the clumsy show!

The tide thinks it's funny,
To tickle my sandy toes,
Kidding, I'll get you!

Jellyfish with flair,
Bouncing like they own the place,
Floaters with no care.

Sheltered Shores of the Heart

Sandcastles stand tall,
But the waves come with a laugh,
"Not your day, my friend."

Crabs in tiny suits,
Marching like they own the shore,
What a shellfish lot!

Kids chasing the tide,
Slip and slide, their giggles soar,
Endless summer fun.

A beach ball takes flight,
Bouncing off a seagull's head,
Hey, come back with that!

Adrift in Celestial Waters

Stars wobble above,
Floating dreams in a small boat,
I forgot my oars.

Turtles in bow ties,
Sipping tea with the moon's glow,
Making time for mates.

The sun teases clouds,
"Not today, oh fluffy friends!"
It's a weather game.

Laughter lingers here,
As dolphins dance through the night,
Who's winning tonight?

Beneath the Caress of Saltwater

Splashing around, I lose my shoe,
Crabs dance around, oh what a view!
Waves tickle toes and laugh with glee,
Fish peek out like they're watching me.

My towel's a ship, it sails on sand,
While seagulls plot, their heists all planned.
A sunburned nose, a target so bright,
Under the sun, I'm quite the sight!

Ice cream drips, I'm covered in goo,
Seashells I find, but none fit my shoe.
Salt in my hair, I'm a beach bum crowned,
In this wild paradise, pure joy is found.

Memories on the Tidal Shore

A wave rolls in, splashing my pants,
I'm dodging sprays, it's a comical dance!
Seagulls squawk, like they're calling my name,
This beach party's a whimsical game.

The sand's a cake, I'm the chef today,
With a shovel in hand, I'm making my way.
Buckets and castles, oh what a sight,
Till the tide sweeps in, it's a grand old fight!

Sunburned and laughing, I juggle my hat,
Once on my head, now a ship's welcome mat.
With friends by my side, the mirth flows like wine,
Memories made near the shoreline's design.

Heartstrings Pulled by the Tide

The tide pulls in, and so do my snacks,
With chips on my lap, I'll dodge the sea hacks.
A wave crashed down, and my drink took flight,
Now it's swimming, a fishy delight!

I built a fine castle, it stood straight and proud,
Until a rogue wave said, 'Hey, look at me now!'
All my hard work washed away in a flash,
The ocean just grinned, oh, that cheeky splash!

I wore my new shades, they're perfect and sleek,
Until a breeze sent them to seek their peak.
In comedy, chaos and laughter we trust,
As we frolic in waves, it's friendship or bust!

Threads of Light in the Surf

Under the sun, I twirl around,
My flip-flops fly; they're nowhere to be found!
Colors of towels like flags in a war,
Everywhere laughter, with smiles galore.

Buried in sand, I'm a mermaid so grand,
But my buddy's beside me, with a foot in hand.
The surf curls up, trying to tickle my feet,
Yet, I'm howling with joy, this day is a treat!

The sun sets low, streaks gold in my hair,
I'm covered in sunscreen, no worry or care.
Threads of light sparkle as night takes its cue,
And I dream of tomorrow, with adventures anew.

Echoes of the Salted Breeze

The waves whisper secrets, oh so sly,
They tickle the sands, then laugh as they fly.
A gull with a joke, in flight, takes a dive,
While crabs hold a meeting, quite jive and alive.

The fish in the tide wear hats of seaweed,
While jellyfish giggle, 'No rules, just our creed!'
A seal plays piano on rocks smooth and gray,
With octopuses clapping, they join in the play.

Secrets Beneath the Azure Veil

Bubbles rise up, with a pop and a cheer,
A clam's got a tale that it won't share here.
Starfish are busy on their lazy stroll,
Saying 'Life's a beach!', it's their casual goal.

Anemones sway, like they're dancing in sync,
While turtles discuss, over seaweed, they drink.
The sea cucumbers gossip, oh what a sight,
They're known as the critters of the deep gossip night.

Cradle of the Endless Deep

Fish in tuxedos waltz in the coral,
While sea urchins giggle, saying, 'Oh, moral!'
A dolphin named Phil plays fetch with a cap,
And loses his ball to a crafty sea lap.

Seahorses prance in a fashion parade,
With snails as their fans, never feeling dismayed.
While narwhals tell tales of the waves they've crossed,
And claim that their tusks are quite stylishly glossed.

Murmurs of the Serene Current

A crab with a stash of shiny things bold,
Claims treasure's the secret to stories retold.
While rays glide past, smooth as butter on bread,
And boast of their journeys, with elegance fed.

In kelp forests lively, the sea otters play,
With laughter and bubbles, they brighten the day.
Surfers ride waves, making fish roll their eyes,
As dolphins dive deep, oh, what a surprise!

Emotions Carried on the High Seas

Waves are giggling, making a fuss,
Seagulls are smirking, causing a buzz.
Fish wear bow ties, swimming in style,
Jellyfish dance, oh what a while!

Salty breezes tickle my nose,
Shells telling secrets, who really knows?
Crabs wearing hats wander about,
Finding their way, but what's that about?

A dolphin leaps in a sassy twist,
Mermaids chuckle, they can't resist.
Every splash is a joke in disguise,
While barnacles giggle, oh how they rise!

So let's ride the waves with a grin so wide,
With laughter as bright as the sunlit tide.
For in this chaos, joy's the decree,
On this whimsical journey, wild and free!

Driftwood Tales and Pebble Memories

Driftwood whispers, tales of old,
Pebbles giggle, if truth be told.
Each piece a story, sandy and grand,
As they play tag with a child on the sand.

Starfish grinning with arms spread wide,
Paddling around, they take a ride.
Seashells are sneaky, hiding their loot,
While octopuses juggle their own little boot.

The tides murmur secrets, giggling away,
As crabs play poker, oh what a play!
Barnacle buddies gather 'round tight,
Sharing tall tales under the moonlight.

So gather your driftwood and pebbles near,
Laugh with the ocean, let go of your fear.
For in the heart of the waves so blue,
There's joy and laughter waiting for you!

Heartbeats in the Eye of the Current

Currents are winking, oh, what a show,
Fish with bright fins swim fast and slow.
Whirls of laughter, bubbles that pop,
Kelp twirls around like a funny backdrop.

Seaspray giggles as it lands on the deck,
While sea turtles glance, giving a peck.
Jellybean jellyfish float with glee,
Wiggling their tentacles, come dance with me!

Whales humming tunes as they dive and swirl,
Sharks acting shy with a humorous twirl.
Seagulls performing a comedic flight,
While anchors drop with a comedic might.

So ride the waves, let your heart be free,
In the playful tide, find your glee.
For amidst the splashes and currents bright,
Laughter echoes, a pure delight!

The Silent Language of Waves

Waves whisper softly, secrets they share,
Creepy crabs skitter, unaware of the flair.
Barnacles chuckle on rocks by the shore,
As fish throw parties, oh, we want more!

The tide tells jokes in a splashy tone,
While starfish giggle, feeling right at home.
Seashells collect laughs like they collect sand,
With each tiny ripple, an oceanic band.

Salty air dances, teasing our hair,
As dolphins dive down without a care.
Even the seaweed joins in the fun,
Wobbling around, not done till it's done!

So toast with your seashell, let's raise a cheer,
For the waves are alive, keep them near.
In their silent laughter, we find our way,
To join in the mirth of the bright ocean play!

The Horizon's Embrace in Marshmallow Skies

Beneath the skies of sticky cream,
The horizon waves, a funny dream.
Seagulls joke with glee in flight,
While sandcastles grow with all their might.

The sun's a marshmallow, puffy and round,
Tickling toes that wander the ground.
Waves giggle softly, tickling the shore,
As flip-flops dance, longing for more.

A crab struts by with a sassy frown,
Wearing its shell like a fancy crown.
While dolphins play tag in a bubbly spree,
They whisper fun secrets, just for me.

Under cotton clouds, we laugh and play,
Time slips like sand, fading away.
With each sunset, our smiles grow wide,
In this silly world, where joy can't hide.

Waters that Hold a Heartfelt Whisper.

Waves chuckle softly, secrets unfold,
With tidal tales, both silly and bold.
Octopuses juggling, a comical sight,
While fish share a joke, bubbling with delight.

The tide rolls in, wearing a goofy grin,
Whispers of laughter where it's been.
Crabs on parade, marching in line,
Stealing the show, feeling just fine.

Seagulls squawk, dressed in hats of foam,
Claiming the beach as their whimsical home.
With every splash, giggles abound,
In a world of whimsy, joy can be found.

Waves bow and sway, a soft comrade,
In this watery jest, we're happily laid.
The rhythm of laughter, the dance of the tide,
In waters that hold joy, we take the ride.

Whispers of the Tidal Embrace

In the morning sun, the tides whisper low,
With jokes in the breeze that only we know.
Nautical nonsense drifts through the waves,
Where sea creatures dance, and mischief behaves.

A fish flips a tale, totally absurd,
As laughter ripples, it feels like a herd.
The seaweed sways, a humorous sway,
Tickling the toes, making them play.

Barnacles nursing a grumpy frown,
Bark back at waves, refusing to drown.
With each gentle splash, the giggles ignite,
In this playful world, everything feels right.

So let's grab our buckets, let's fill up with cheer,
With whispers of joy, there's nothing to fear.
In the arms of the tide, we laugh, we sing,
Together we jest, oh, the joy we bring.

Ocean's Gentle Lullaby

Hush now, listen, the ocean sings,
A lullaby woven with whimsical strings.
Waves sway softly, in rhythm and rhyme,
Knitting together the fabric of time.

From jellyfish parties to dolphins that race,
The sea's not a place for a serious face.
Shells play the drums, while sea stars clap,
Creating a concert that makes us all tap.

A whale tells jokes with a deep, booming sound,
While fish spin around, in circles they bound.
The soft serenade of the rolling tide,
Where giggles and gurgles happily bide.

So close your eyes, let the waves be your guide,
In this lullaby, let laughter abide.
With every soft crash, find dreams so sweet,
In the ocean's embrace, where fun and love meet.

Ocean Dances: Adagio of the Deep

In the water, fish take a bow,
Seagulls giggle; take your vow!
Wave your fins, let's start the show,
As crabs in tuxedos dance below.

Octopuses twist in grand ballet,
While starfish simply sit and sway.
Even the coral joins the fun,
Who knew the ocean could play and run?

Turtles glide like they own the floor,
Splashing joy from the ocean's core.
Every wave whispers jokes so bright,
Under the moon's soft silvery light.

Join the dance, don't miss your chance,
The ocean's giggles, a merry trance.
With your floaties, take a leap,
In water's laughter, dive in deep!

The Caress of Brine on Sunkiest Skin

An otter snags a sun-soaked snack,
While lifeguards wear flip-flops, that's a fact!
Seashells gossip in rustling waves,
Meanwhile, dolphins impersonate knaves.

A jellyfish juggles with zero care,
Waving goodbye to a sunburned hair.
Sandcastles tumble with boisterous glee,
"Forgive my flop," they say with a plea.

Crabs strut sideways, a funny parade,
Dancing in rhythm—though they're quite afraid.
Seagulls steal fries like it's their job,
The beach is a stage for each sneaky mob!

Saltwater kisses leave a silly grin,
Laughing all day until the night's thin.
In sunlit frolic, everyone basks,
While finding true joy is all that one asks.

Reflections in the Aquamarine Radiance

Look at fish sporting shades divine,
Reflecting colors; oh, what a sign!
Squid in a tux takes a silly spin,
While anchovies laugh, 'Let's all dive in!'

The surface shines like a game of tag,
Each ripple resounds with a playful brag.
Mermaids grin with bubblegum flair,
As dolphins giggle at seaweed fair.

Floaties bob like they've hitched a ride,
Jellybeans tumble in glee, open wide.
With the tide rises a contagious cheer,
Where every splash calls for friends to appear!

The sunlight winks through the aqua beams,
Water's reflections are full of dreams.
Let's play pirates, or maybe just float,
The ocean's humor; an endless anecdote!

A Canvas of Dreams on the Waters

A fish flops featured in fuzzy hues,
Sporting an art that would spark good views.
Clams critique with a pearl to share,
While turtles paint without a care.

Brush strokes of bubbles, colors collide,
Whales hum tunes with sound waves wide.
Canvas of water holds laughter tight,
With jests and chuckles, a glorious sight!

The sand grins back in playful jest,
Even the wind wants to join the fest.
Painted horizons all shine with mirth,
In this water world of joyous birth.

Splash on more color, let humor swell,
An ocean of giggles; who can tell?
In this gallery of waterfalls bright,
Where nature smiles, it feels so right!

Tranquil Depths of the Indigo Deep

Bubbles rise, fish take flight,
Doing flips in morning light,
Octopus dances, a silly spree,
Who knew they'd sip on cups of tea?

Seagulls squawk, they wear a frown,
As the tide pulls their snacks down,
Crabs in a race, pinching away,
Who knew they were such fans of ballet?

Jellyfish float, oh so bizarre,
Glow in the dark like a disco star,
Mermaids gossip about the breeze,
While dolphins laugh beneath the trees.

Waves crash high, "What a splash!" they say,
Making sandcastles wash away,
In the indigo, secrets play,
Turns out, sea life loves a café!

The Ocean's Tender Reverie

Turtles do the moonwalk, what a sight,
While starfish chill, soaking up the night,
Seahorses play hopscotch on the sand,
Who knew they'd form a rock band?

The tide comes in with a cheerful grin,
Making sure all the fun can begin,
Clams keep secrets, pearls hidden away,
"Trust us, it's just another cliché!"

Squid with sunglasses strut on the shore,
Telling jokes that leave us wanting more,
Splashes of laughter as waves roll through,
With a pinch of salt, laughter ensues!

Stars twinkle softly; the ocean sleeps,
Dreaming of friends and making peeps,
In a reverie of playful cheer,
Ocean whispers, "I wish you were here!"

Surrendering to the Rhythm of the Surf

Waves crash and tumble, a dance we share,
With fish in tuxedos, swimming with flair,
A clam checked the tide for a fashion show,
"Do you think this shell makes my outfit glow?"

Seagulls pirouette, diving down low,
While crabs hold a meeting on who stole the show,
"Was it you, Mr. Shrimp?" they're quick to accuse,
But he just winks, "I'll always amuse!"

Surfboards zoom, riding the swell,
Shark's on the side, 'Don't break the spell!'
They chit and they chatter; the ocean's a stage,
With laughter and joy, we're all at this age.

Under the sunset, the day takes a bow,
As creatures retire, not knowing how,
The rhythm of waves brings laughter galore,
"Catch you tomorrow; there's always more!"

Moods of the Moonlit Abyss

In the moonlight, crabs with sunglasses shine,
Dance their tango, feeling just fine,
Fish gossip under corals so bright,
"What's that noise? Is it dance night?"

Manta rays glide like sheets on the breeze,
While squids take selfies, channeling ease,
The ocean's a stage, a curious mess,
With jellyfish lighting up to impress.

Whales join in with notes that delight,
Harmonizing softly, a musical night,
"Is that Neptune?" one fish jokes with glee,
"No, just my cousin, did you see?"

Shining and sparkling, waves join the fun,
As laughter echoes beneath the moon run,
In the abyss, all creatures unite,
With gleeful whispers, "We'll do it tonight!"

Dreams Adrift on a Serene Horizon

Big waves dance like clumsy friends,
Splashing laughs that never end.
A jellyfish wearing a goofy grin,
Waves goodbye as I dive in.

Seagulls squawk a silly song,
They swoop and dive, where they belong.
With sandy toes and salty hair,
Who needs worries? I haven't a care.

The sun brings warmth, a fishy smell,
A crab does cartwheels, oh so well.
Its tiny legs and wobbly gait,
Make me giggle, it's truly great.

Among the shells, I find a pearl,
It rolls away, a playful whirl.
Chasing treasures, I can't be caught,
In this funny world, laughter is sought.

Currents of Compassion in Liquid Blue

The waves chuckle with gentle tease,
Bubbles giggle, moving with ease.
A floppy whale flicks its tail high,
Squirting water, oh my, oh my!

Starfish grinning, stuck on a rock,
Tickled by a passing flock.
A fish in a tie, struts on by,
Winking at shells, does he even try?

Gulls play poker, they squawk and dive,
Betting on the seaweed to thrive.
With every card, a splash and a shout,
Joining the fun, there's never a doubt.

Beneath the sun, in playful cheer,
The ocean's charm is oh so clear.
In every wave, a chuckle's found,
In this watery world, silliness abounds.

Beneath the Surface: A Hidden Warmth

The octopus wears a tiny hat,
It squeezes through cracks, imagine that!
With eight arms, it waves hello,
Dancing away with a dazzling show.

Tiny fish in a line do play,
Chasing each other all day today.
Each little splash, a burst of fun,
In a watery world where the laughter's spun.

A clam that opens, oh what surprise,
Revealing a joke in all its guise.
"You crack me up!" it laughs out loud,
Joining the sea, what a silly crowd.

Bubbles rise up, a fizzy cheer,
Tickling toes, they disappear.
In the depths, a warmth does flow,
A giggle here, a chuckle below.

A Symphony of Shells and Stars

Seashells sing a funny tune,
Under the watchful eye of the moon.
With rhythms of tides that twist and whirl,
They flap their edges, they hop and swirl.

Starfish gather for a dance, oh what glee,
Twirling patterns in water, wild and free.
Each point a move, it's quite surreal,
A star-studded ocean, what a fun-filled reel.

Sand castles built with a bucket and spade,
Toppled by waves, but never dismayed.
"Build it again!" cries a mermaid with flair,
Who tickles the sand with a flip of her hair.

As night descends, the stars twinkle bright,
Each one a laugh, a spark in the night.
In this realm, where giggles unfold,
The ocean's jests are endlessly told.

A Haven in the Seafoam Shadows

In the shadows where the foam plays,
Light dances in a silly haze.
Crabs wear hats and dance around,
While seagulls mimic silly sounds.

Jellyfish flash with colors bright,
A party under the pale moonlight.
Fishy friends with goofy grins,
Splashing water, where joy begins.

Seaweed sways like it's in a trance,
Inviting all to join the dance.
Starfish twirl with all their might,
In this haven, all feels right.

Laughter bubbles with each wave's crest,
A playful place, we are so blessed.
In the seafoam shadows we float,
On a giggle, we'll happily gloat.

The Calm After the Storm's Whisper

After the tempest, all is still,
The ocean murmurs, what a thrill!
Seashells giggle in the sand,
As waves tickle, oh so grand.

The clouds drift by with sleepy yawns,
While dolphins play from dusk till dawn.
A wave hits hard, then rolls away,
It leaves us laughing, come what may.

Rainbows stretch, a smiling bow,
Over waters that giggle low.
No need to worry, just hold tight,
The calm brings joy, it's pure delight.

With every ripple, a joke is spun,
Ocean's laughter under the sun.
Who knew the deep could be so bright?
In a storm's calm, we find our light.

Reflections in the Ocean's Eye

In the water's gaze, a winking grin,
Reflecting tales where mirth begins.
Pirates laugh, they swing and sway,
Chasing treasures that run away.

Mermaids sing their silly song,
As fish join in, they all belong.
A crab with glasses reads a book,
While starfish jump from nook to nook.

The tides hold secrets, oh so neat,
Underwater shoes for dancing feet.
Bubbles rise like giggling friends,
In the eye of the ocean, the fun never ends.

As twilight falls, the moon beams bright,
With silver sparkles, oh what a sight!
In reflections, joy we'll find,
In the ocean's gaze, we're intertwined.

Journey of the Softest Tides

Upon the waves, we set our sails,
Through giggles and some dreamy trails.
Softest tides, where trouble hides,
With every splash, our laughter glides.

Gulls tell tales of merry days,
As we boat along the frothy ways.
A fish in flip-flops takes a stroll,
While crabs play tag, oh, what a goal!

Bobbing along, nothing is dire,
With each wave, we feel the fire.
The ocean sways, a gentle hug,
In this journey, we all feel snug.

As tides retreat and then return,
With newfound joy, the sea will churn.
On the softest tides, we glide and play,
In a watery world, foolish and gay.

Soliloquy of the Sandy Cove

Oh, the sand tickles my toes,
As the waves giggle and pose.
Seagulls squawk like they own the scene,
While crabs pinch in their tiny marine.

Buckets and shovels ore in tow,
Building castles with the hope they'll grow.
But the tide laughs and washes them down,
Leaving just memories, not a crown.

The sun plays hide-and-seek with my hat,
While dolphins swim like they're in a spat.
Each splash and splash a comedic scene,
With fish waving fins, feeling quite keen.

So here I sit with a cocktail in hand,
While sea foam frolics upon the sand.
Nature chuckles in this salty retreat,
In every wave, a joke to repeat.

Wings of the Wind's Children

Feathers from heaven give a flutter,
As winds blow through, making things utter.
Kites dance above like they're on a spree,
Chasing the clouds, feeling so free.

The breeze brings whispers, secrets abound,
While children giggle, joy unbound.
They run and tumble, racing the gust,
In this airy playground, laughter is a must.

Tails of the kites wave like they're alive,
In this game of tags where imaginations thrive.
Even the sun grins with beams so bright,
As the day fades, a glorious sight.

Each dip and dive a comic charade,
As shadows stretch, crisp colors fade.
With every gust, a new tale to weave,
With wings of the wind, we believe.

The Ocean's Hidden Embrace

Beneath the waves, what wonders hide,
With fish that dance, oh what a ride!
An octopus starts a game of chance,
Revealing tricks with each sly glance.

A turtle with glasses grumbles and sighs,
While jellyfish float like they're in disguise.
Seashells gossip, their stories to tell,
In bubbly whispers, they're under a spell.

The oysters chuckle, slapped by a tide,
While starfish twirl with the currents beside.
Even the seaweed joins in the fun,
Twisting and turning 'til the day is done.

So dive down deep, if you dare,
For laughter and mischief linger somewhere.
In the deep blue where the silliness flows,
The ocean's embrace, a sitcom that glows.

A Conch's Whispering Secrets

A conch shell perched high on a rock,
Claims to have secrets it'll gladly unlock.
With every turn, it spills out a tale,
Of love and laughter, of storms, and of sail.

"Listen closely," it tenderly sighs,
"Fishes have dreams, and dolphins have ties.
The current once raced a determined crab,
But alas, ended up in a seaweed nab!"

With bubble-laden giggles, it shares its scope,
Of pirate ghosts and underwater hope.
Eels in tuxedos, swaying with glee,
All waltzing 'round like a grand jubilee!

So, hold it near, this magical shell,
It spins funny stories, Oh, so well!
For in each whisper lies humor unbound,
The conch's laugh travels, all around.

Embracing the Ocean's Pulse

The waves tickle toes, oh what a game,
Splashing and laughing, no one's to blame.
A crab in a tux, quite dapper and sly,
Waving his claws, just passing by.

Fish flash their smiles in a bubbly parade,
Making their way through the seaweed cascade.
Seagulls play tag with a bright beach ball,
While dolphins dive in for the joyful call.

Jellyfish waltz in an elegant dance,
Ah, feel the rhythm—come join the chance!
But watch where you step, dear friend, don't you slip,
Or find yourself on a very wet trip!

With sand in your shorts, you laugh at the tide,
As it wraps all your worries like a sea-salted ride.
Life's a light splash, with giggles galore,
So embrace every wave, oh what fun's in store!

Glistening Scales of Serendipity

In a bright coral dress, the fish love to flirt,
While turtles wear shades, looking stylish, not hurt.
Octopus chefs whip up a bubblegum stew,
As sea cucumbers giggle—who knew?

Starfish on duty, they think they're so grand,
Striking a pose, like a rock band in sand.
A clam holds a secret, oh what could it be?
'My pearls are rare gems!' they boast to the sea.

The shrimp have a party, with dance moves so slick,
While anchovies chant, "We're not just a trick!"
They twirl through the currents, all shiny and bright,
Who knew underwater could be such a sight?

Oh, the fish tell tall tales of adventures so wacky,
With each little splash, they feel oh-so-hacky.
In this splashy world, laughter reigns supreme,
With glistening scales, it's a floaty daydream!

Eternity's Breath in Slow Motion

When waves roll in slow, like a sleepy old cat,
They curl by your feet, as if saying, "How's that?"
A starfish blows kisses, oh darling so sweet,
While anemones wiggle and dance to the beat.

The sun takes a nap on the ocean's warm back,
And surfboards drift by on this languid track.
A sailor in swimsuits, an odd fashion fit,
Claims he's found treasure—just a half-eaten kit!

Sea otters lounge, with their cute furry toys,
They chuckle and giggle like squeaky-voiced boys.
Time moves like molasses, with seashells on deck,
And laughter's the anchor, no reason to wreck.

So let's twirl in the foam, under sun's gentle grace,
With every slow wave, find your smile in this place.
In eternity's breath, let the merriment flow,
For life's but a dance in this ebbing show!

The Gentle Tide's Serenade

The tide sings a song, soft and warm on the beach,
As seashells keep rhythm, just out of reach.
A quirky old crab raps with rhythm and rhyme,
Telling tales of his youth, oh what a good time!

Waves whisper secrets to sandcastles grand,
"Don't worry, dear friends, we'll hold up our stand!"
Gulls swoop and dive, with a laugh in their call,
As the sun-drenched horizon begins its nightfall.

A dolphin comes dancing, a splash of delight,
Tickling the bubbles in water's soft light.
"Let's throw a luau!" calls the fish in the tide,
And soon, every swimmer joins in the ride!

So come take a dip in this gentle embrace,
Where laughter and joy fill this magical space.
For in every wave, there's a story to spin,
With the tide's gentle serenade, let the fun begin!

The Ocean's Unseen Affection

When waves play a game of tag,
They splash on rocks with a laugh.
Fish swim by, donning a grin,
Even crabs dance with a staff.

Seaweed sways like a silly hat,
Starfish wave with a chill.
Bubbles pop, a cheerful sound,
The tide brings joy with goodwill.

A Composed Symphony of Blue

Shells whistle tunes as they rest,
While seagulls croon from above.
The dolphin's jokes are the best,
As they bounce with a joke of love.

The octopus plays a sly trick,
Changing colors in a flash.
With ink and giggles, it's slick,
A grand old watery bash!

Rippling Inklings of Love

Little waves whisper sweet nicknames,
For seashells and rocks on the shore.
Turtles attempt crazy games,
While crabs keep score, wanting more.

Whales sing softly, a jest in their song,
As they barrel roll with glee.
Even the squid can't help but long,
For a joke that's fishy and free!

The Quiet Anthem of the Deep

At dusk, the fish plot a parade,
With fins as their festive attire.
They twirl and spin – oh, what a charade!
And dolphins light up for hire.

The quiet eel in a tuxedo bold,
Whispers secrets to the night.
While starfish share tales of the old,
In the moon's glowing light.

Serenade of Waves In Bloom

Waves dance like they own the day,
Bubbles popping in a playful way.
Seagulls giggle, making a fuss,
As fish flash smiles on their big bus.

Shells play music from sandy shores,
Crabs join in like happy chore.
Sandcastles wobble with every cheer,
While starfish wink, they're in on the joke here.

Laughter echoes through the blue,
As tides hitch rides on skies anew.
Jellyfish float with a jelly bean grin,
Inviting all to join in the din.

So hop along this jolly spree,
Where the silliness flows, wild and free.
Each wave a prank, each tide a jest,
Under the sun, they laugh at their best.

The Coral's Tender Caress

Corals giggle in layers of hue,
Tickling fish that swim right through.
A clownfish juggles with a grin wide,
While octopuses try to hide inside.

Anemones wave like they're in a band,
Inviting all critters to take a stand.
A crab in a tuxedo struts quite bold,
While seaweed sways, a sight to behold.

Tiny shrimp laugh at the feathered show,
As dolphins play tag with a throw of foam.
Each coral corner holds a jest,
Beneath the waves, it's all a fest.

So join the fun in this vibrant place,
Where every creature has a face.
In a world of laughter under sunlit skies,
A treasure trove of giggles and fun surprises!

Beneath the Horizon's Gaze

Beneath the sky, horizons tease,
With winking clouds that flirt like breeze.
Dolphins dive in playful flair,
Surfing waves without a care.

A turtle wearing shades rolls by,
While a parrotfish, oh my oh my!
Sings ballads to the passing schools,
As sunlight sparkles, breaking the rules.

Whales tell jokes in booming sings,
As water splashes and laughter rings.
The horizon giggles out loud and bright,
In a sea of joy that feels just right.

So come along and take a peek,
At every wave that plays hide-and-seek.
With each splash, let mirth take flight,
Under the realm of pure delight.

Shelters of Tempest's Tears

When storms bumble in like a clumsy kid,
The waves all giggle, 'Oh, let's play hid!'
Raindrops dance like they've had too much,
Splashing about with a bubbly touch.

Thunder rumbles like a funny joke,
While lightning flashes give a fun poke.
Clouds play tag over the choppy sea,
In this tempest's tale, let's all be free.

But once they settle, the calm appears,
Revealing joy from tempest's tears.
With rainbows blooming in goofy arcs,
And every wave offering cheeky sparks.

So remember, storms may seem quite rough,
But in their wake, it's all silly stuff.
In the ocean's heart, laughter proclaims,
Every drop a giggle - life's little games.

www.ingramcontent.com/pod-product-compliance
Lightning Source LLC
Chambersburg PA
CBHW060145230426
43661CB00003B/576